Better Homes and Gardens

Shortcut Cookies

Our seal assures you that every recipe in *Shortcut Cookies*
has been tested in the Better Homes and Gardens® Test Kitchen.
This means that each recipe is practical and reliable,
and meets our high standards of taste appeal.

Peanut Butter and Chocolate Chip Bars

The cake mix gives you a head start.

1 **package 2-layer-size
white cake mix**
½ **cup peanut butter**
2 **tablespoons margarine
or butter, softened**
1 **egg**
¼ **cup milk**
1 **3-ounce package cream
cheese, cut up**
¼ **cup sugar**
¼ **cup unsweetened cocoa
powder**
2 **eggs**
1 **teaspoon vanilla**
1 **6-ounce package
(1 cup) semisweet
chocolate pieces**
½ **cup chopped peanuts**

Set aside *¾ cup* of the dry cake mix. For crust, in a large mixing bowl stir together peanut butter and margarine or butter. Beat in 1 egg and milk. Stir in the remaining cake mix till combined. Press onto the bottom of a greased 13x9x2-inch baking pan. Bake in a 350° oven for 10 minutes.

Meanwhile, in a small mixer bowl beat cream cheese till softened. Add sugar and cocoa powder. Mix till combined. Add the 2 eggs and vanilla; beat till smooth. Beat in the reserved ¾ cup cake mix. Stir in chocolate pieces and peanuts. Drop by spoonfuls atop baked crust. Carefully spread over the crust. Bake in the 350° oven about 15 minutes or till surface springs back when lightly touched. Cool on a wire rack. Cut into bars while warm. Makes 36 bars.

Toffee Brownies

6 **1⅛-ounce bars
chocolate-covered
English toffee**
1 **20.5-ounce package
brownie mix**

Crush toffee bars. Stir together brownie mix and *half* of the crushed toffee bars. Prepare according to the brownie package directions. Sprinkle remaining crushed toffee bars atop. Bake according to package directions. Cool on a wire rack. Makes 24 bars.

Date Brownies

Made with only four ingredients.

1 **20.5-ounce package brownie mix**
1 **cup pitted whole dates, snipped**
½ **cup chopped walnuts Sifted powdered sugar**

Stir together the brownie mix, dates, and chopped walnuts. Prepare according to the brownie package directions. Bake according to the package directions. Cool completely on a wire rack. Sprinkle with sifted powdered sugar. Makes 24 bars.

Maple-Coconut Bars

Our taste panel loved the rich chewiness of these simple bars.

1⅓ **cups coconut**
¼ **cup margarine *or* butter**
¾ **cup all-purpose flour**
¾ **cup sugar**
1 **egg**
½ **teaspoon baking powder**
½ **teaspoon maple flavoring**
¼ **teaspoon salt**
¼ **cup chopped walnuts**
1 **tablespoon margarine *or* butter, melted**

Reserve *½ cup* of the coconut for topping. Finely chop the remaining coconut. In a mixer bowl beat the ¼ cup margarine or butter about 30 seconds or till softened. Add *¼ cup* of the flour, sugar, egg, baking powder, maple flavoring, and salt. Beat for 1 to 2 minutes or till well mixed. Add remaining flour; beat till combined.

Stir in the chopped coconut and walnuts. Spread in a greased 8x8x2-inch baking pan. Stir together the reserved coconut and 1 tablespoon melted margarine or butter. Sprinkle over mixture in the pan. Bake in a 350° oven about 30 minutes or till top is golden and a wooden toothpick inserted in center comes out clean. Cool on a wire rack. Makes 24 bars.

Mocha-Cinnamon Fingers

2 teaspoons instant
   coffee crystals
½ teaspoon vanilla
1 cup margarine *or* butter
2 cups all-purpose flour
½ cup sugar
½ cup packed brown
   sugar
1 egg yolk
1 teaspoon ground
   cinnamon
1 cup semisweet
   chocolate pieces
1 cup walnuts *or* pecans

Stir together coffee crystals, vanilla, and ½ teaspoon *water* till coffee crystals dissolve. In a mixer bowl beat margarine or butter about 30 seconds or till softened. Add *1 cup* of the flour, sugar, brown sugar, egg yolk, cinnamon, and coffee mixture. Beat on low speed for 1 to 2 minutes or till well mixed. Add remaining flour. Beat till combined. Press mixture into an ungreased 15x10x1-inch baking pan. Bake in a 350° oven for 15 to 18 minutes or till light brown and starting to pull away from edges. Immediately sprinkle with chocolate pieces. Let stand till the chocolate softens. Evenly spread chocolate over the top. Finely chop nuts; sprinkle atop. Cool slightly. Cut into bars while warm. Makes 48 bars.

Rocky Road Brownies

1 cup semisweet
   chocolate pieces
⅓ cup margarine *or* butter
1 cup all-purpose flour
¾ cup sugar
2 eggs
1 teaspoon vanilla
½ teaspoon baking
   powder
½ cup tiny marshmallows
¼ cup chopped nuts

Heat and stir *½ cup* of the chocolate pieces over low heat till melted. Remove from heat and cool slightly. Beat margarine or butter about 30 seconds or till softened. Add *½ cup* of the flour, sugar, eggs, vanilla, baking powder, and melted chocolate. Beat till well mixed. Add remaining flour; beat till combined. Spread in a greased 9x9x2-inch baking pan. Bake in a 350° oven for 20 minutes. Sprinkle with remaining chocolate pieces, marshmallows, and nuts. Bake for 3 to 5 minutes more or till chocolate pieces just begin to melt. Cool on a wire rack. Makes 24 bars.

Clockwise, on plate, from top: Mocha-Cinnamon Fingers, Oatmeal and Jam Bars, Rocky Road Brownies, and Craters of Coconut (see recipe, page 23).

Oatmeal and Jam Bars

1⅓ cups all-purpose flour
¾ cup quick-cooking rolled oats
⅓ cup packed brown sugar
1 teaspoon finely shredded lemon peel
¼ teaspoon baking soda
2 3-ounce packages cream cheese
¼ cup margarine *or* butter
¾ cup peach jam
1 teaspoon lemon juice

In a mixing bowl stir together flour, oats, brown sugar, lemon peel, baking soda, and ¼ teaspoon *salt.* Cut in cream cheese and margarine or butter till mixture is crumbly. Set aside 1 cup of the mixture.

Pat the remaining oat mixture onto the bottom of a greased 9x9x2-inch baking pan. Bake in a 350° oven for 20 minutes. Meanwhile, stir together jam and lemon juice. Spread over baked layer. Sprinkle with the reserved oat mixture. Bake in the 350° oven about 15 minutes more or till golden. Cool completely on a wire rack. Makes 36 bars.

Chocolate Chip and Pumpkin Bars

A little like a cake and a little like a cookie, this bar combines the best of both sweets.

4 beaten eggs
1 16-ounce can (2 cups)
    pumpkin
1½ cups sugar
¼ cup cooking oil
¼ cup milk
2 teaspoons baking
    powder
2 teaspoons pumpkin
    pie spice
1 teaspoon baking soda
1 teaspoon salt
2 cups all-purpose flour
1 6-ounce package
    (1 cup) semisweet
    chocolate pieces,
    one 6-ounce package
    (1 cup) miniature
    semisweet chocolate
    pieces, *or* 1 cup
    raisins
1 can cream cheese
    frosting *or* sifted
    powdered sugar
    (optional)

In a mixing bowl stir together eggs, pumpkin, sugar, cooking oil, milk, baking powder, pumpkin pie spice, soda, and salt. Stir in flour just till moistened. Stir in chocolate pieces or raisins.

Spread in an ungreased 15x10x1-inch baking pan. Bake in a 350° oven for 25 to 30 minutes or till top springs back when lightly touched. Cool completely on a wire rack. Frost with cream cheese frosting or sprinkle with sifted powdered sugar, if desired. Makes 36 bars.

Pecan-Pie Bars

1½ cups all-purpose flour
  2 tablespoons brown
     sugar
  ½ cup margarine *or* butter
  2 eggs
  ½ cup packed brown
     sugar
  ½ cup chopped pecans
  ½ cup corn syrup
  2 tablespoons margarine
     or butter, melted
  1 teaspoon vanilla

Stir together flour and 2 tablespoons brown sugar. Cut in the ½ cup margarine or butter till mixture resembles coarse crumbs. Pat onto the bottom of an ungreased 11x7x1½-inch baking pan. Bake in a 350° oven for 15 minutes.

In a mixing bowl beat eggs slightly. Stir in ½ cup brown sugar, pecans, corn syrup, 2 tablespoons margarine or butter, and vanilla. Pour over baked layer. Bake in the 350° oven about 20 to 25 minutes more or till center is set. Cool slightly on a wire rack. Cut into bars while warm. Makes 32 bars.

Praline Bars

1¾ cups all-purpose flour
  ⅓ cup packed brown
     sugar
  1 teaspoon baking
     powder
  ¾ cup margarine *or* butter
  2 eggs
  ¼ cup praline liqueur
     or brandy
  2 cups sifted powdered
     sugar
  2 cups broken pecans
 36 pecan halves

For crust, stir together flour, brown sugar, baking powder, and ¼ teaspoon *salt*. Cut in margarine till mixture resembles coarse crumbs. In a mixing bowl beat together *one* of the eggs and *2 tablespoons* of the liqueur. Stir into the flour mixture. Press onto the bottom of a greased 13x9x2-inch baking pan.

Stir together remaining egg and remaining liqueur. Stir in powdered sugar and the 2 cups pecans. Spread over the crust. Arrange pecan halves on top in six rows of six each. Bake in a 375° oven for 15 to 18 minutes or till center is set. Cool slightly on a wire rack. Cut into bars while warm. Makes 36 bars.

Double-Almond Cookies

Almond paste and sliced almonds make these cookies doubly almondy. (Pictured on page 11.)

¾ **cup margarine** *or* **butter**
1¾ **cups all-purpose flour**
⅔ **cup sugar**
1 **egg**
1 **teaspoon vanilla**
1 **beaten egg**
½ **cup almond paste**
2 **tablespoons sugar**
1 **tablespoon milk**
Sliced almonds

Beat margarine for 30 seconds. Add ¾ *cup* of the flour, ⅔ cup sugar, 1 egg, and vanilla. Beat till mixed. Add remaining flour. Beat till combined. Cover. Chill for 30 minutes. Shape into two 6-inch rolls. Wrap in waxed paper. Chill for several hours or till firm. For topping, beat together 1 egg, almond paste, 2 tablespoons sugar, and milk. Cut dough into ¼-inch-thick slices. Place on ungreased cookie sheets. Spread about *1 teaspoon* topping on *each* cookie. Sprinkle with almonds. Bake in a 375° oven about 10 minutes or till brown. Cool. Makes 48 cookies.

Refrigerator Pecan Cookies

⅓ **cup margarine** *or* **butter**
1¼ **cups all-purpose flour**
½ **cup sugar**
¼ **cup packed brown**
  sugar
1 **egg**
½ **teaspoon vanilla**
¼ **teaspoon baking soda**
¼ **teaspoon salt**
½ **cup finely chopped**
  pecans, toasted

In a mixer bowl beat margarine or butter for 30 seconds. Add ½ *cup* of the flour, sugar, brown sugar, egg, vanilla, baking soda, and salt. Beat till well mixed. Add remaining flour. Beat till combined. Stir in pecans. Cover and chill dough for 1 hour. Shape into two 6-inch rolls. Wrap in waxed paper. Chill for several hours or till firm. (If using margarine, you may need to chill dough in the freezer to make it firm enough to slice.) Cut dough into ¼-inch-thick slices. Place on greased cookie sheets. Bake in a 375° oven about 8 minutes or till light brown. Cool on a wire rack. Makes 48 cookies.

Coconut-Meringue Cookies

Since these cookies don't store well, keep them in an airtight container and only for a day or two.

¾ cup margarine *or* butter
1¾ cups all-purpose flour
⅔ cup sugar
1 egg
1 teaspoon vanilla
⅛ teaspoon ground cinnamon
Dash ground allspice
2 egg whites
1 teaspoon vanilla
⅛ teaspoon cream of tartar
1 cup sugar

Beat margarine for 30 seconds. Add ¾ *cup* of the flour, ⅔ cup sugar, 1 egg, 1 teaspoon vanilla, cinnamon, and allspice. Beat till mixed. Add remaining flour. Beat till combined. Cover. Chill for 30 minutes. Shape into two 6-inch rolls. Wrap in waxed paper. Chill for several hours or till firm. For meringue, beat 2 egg whites, 1 teaspoon vanilla, and cream of tartar till soft peaks form. Gradually add 1 cup sugar, beating till stiff peaks form. Cut dough into ¼-inch-thick slices. Place on ungreased cookie sheets. Pipe or spoon meringue atop each cookie. Sprinkle with coconut, if desired. Bake in a 325° oven for 15 to 18 minutes or till brown. Cool. Makes 48 cookies.

Double-Peanut-Butter Cookies

½ cup margarine *or* butter
½ cup peanut butter
1½ cups all-purpose flour
⅓ cup sugar
⅓ cup packed brown sugar
3 tablespoons orange juice *or* milk
½ teaspoon baking soda
Peanut butter

Beat margarine and ½ cup peanut butter for 30 seconds. Add ¾ *cup* of the flour, sugar, brown sugar, juice, and soda. Beat till mixed. Add remaining flour. Beat till combined. Shape into a 10-inch roll. Wrap in waxed paper. Chill for several hours or till firm. Cut into ⅛-inch-thick slices. Place *half* of the slices on ungreased cookie sheets. Dollop *each* with ½ *teaspoon* peanut butter. Top with remaining slices. Seal edges with a fork. Bake in a 350° oven for 10 to 12 minutes or till firm. Cool. Makes 40 cookies.

Mocha-Nut Rounds

Make two different cookies using just one dough.

2 teaspoons instant
    coffee crystals
½ teaspoon water
¾ cup margarine *or* butter
1¾ cups all-purpose flour
⅔ cup sugar
2 squares (2 ounces)
    semisweet chocolate,
    melted and cooled
1 egg
1 teaspoon vanilla
½ cup milk chocolate
    pieces
1 tablespoon shortening
1 cup pistachio nuts

Dissolve coffee crystals in water. Beat margarine or butter for 30 seconds. Add *¾ cup* of the flour, sugar, 2 squares melted chocolate, egg, vanilla, and coffee mixture. Beat with an electric mixer on low speed till mixed. Add remaining flour. Beat till combined. Cover. Chill for 30 minutes or till firm enough to handle. Shape into two 6-inch rolls. Wrap in waxed paper or clear plastic wrap. Chill for several hours or till firm.

Cut dough into ¼-inch-thick slices. Place on ungreased cookie sheets. Bake in 350° oven for 10 to 12 minutes or till firm. Cool on wire rack. Meanwhile, melt together ½ cup chocolate pieces and shortening. Finely chop nuts. Roll edges of cookies in chocolate mixture, then in nuts. Makes 48 cookies.

Mocha Kisses: Prepare as above, *except* omit the milk chocolate pieces, shortening, and pistachio nuts. After chilling the rolls of dough for several hours, cut each roll in half horizontally to form 4 half-moon-shaped logs. Cut each log into ¼-inch-thick slices. Wrap each slice around one *milk chocolate kiss.* Place on ungreased cookie sheets with chocolate kisses standing upright. Bake in a 350° oven about 10 minutes or till firm. Sprinkle with sifted *powdered sugar.* Cool completely on a wire rack. Makes 96 cookies.

Clockwise from top center: Mocha-Nut Rounds, Brown Sugar and Spice Rounds, Coconut Meringue Cookies (see recipe, page 9), Mocha Kisses, and Double-Almond Cookies (see recipe, page 8).

Brown Sugar and Spice Rounds

¾ cup margarine *or* butter
1¾ cups all-purpose flour
⅔ cup packed brown
    sugar
1 egg
1 teaspoon vanilla
½ teaspoon ground ginger
⅛ teaspoon ground
    cinnamon
⅛ teaspoon ground
    nutmeg
    Dash ground allspice
    Glaze

Beat margarine for 30 seconds. Add ¾ *cup* of the flour, sugar, egg, vanilla, and spices. Beat till mixed. Add remaining flour. Beat till combined. Cover. Chill for 30 minutes. Shape into two 6-inch rolls. Wrap in waxed paper. Chill for several hours or till firm. Cut into ¼-inch-thick slices. Bake on ungreased cookie sheets in a 350° oven for 10 to 12 minutes or till firm. Cool. Drizzle with Glaze. Makes 48 cookies.

Glaze: Melt 2 tablespoons *margarine*. Stir in ¼ cup packed *brown sugar*. Cook and stir till bubbly. Remove from heat. Stir in ½ cup sifted *powdered sugar* and enough *milk* to make of drizzling consistency.

11

Festive Cookie Dough

1 **cup margarine** *or* **butter**
1 **8-ounce package cream cheese**
3½ **cups all-purpose flour**
2 **cups sugar**
1 **egg**
1 **teaspoon baking powder**
1 **teaspoon vanilla**
¼ **teaspoon almond extract (optional)**

In a mixer bowl beat margarine or butter and cream cheese about 30 seconds or till softened. Add *1½ cups* of the flour, sugar, egg, baking powder, vanilla, and, if desired, almond extract. Beat for 1 to 2 minutes or till well mixed. Add remaining flour. Beat till combined. (You may need to stir in the last of the flour by hand.) Divide dough into three portions (about 2 cups each). Cover and chill overnight. *Or,* place in moisture- and vaporproof wrap. Seal, label, and freeze for up to 3 months. Makes 3 portions.

Mint Rounds

1 **portion Festive Cookie Dough (see recipe, above)**
¼ **to ⅓ pound pastel cream mint kisses (36 pieces)**

If frozen, thaw Festive Cookie Dough in the refrigerator overnight. *Or,* place dough in a microwave-safe mixing bowl. Cover with waxed paper. Micro-cook on 10% power (low) about 5 minutes or till thawed, turning dough over once.

On a lightly floured surface, roll chilled or thawed dough to ⅛-inch thickness. Cut with a 2½-inch-round cookie cutter. Place on ungreased cookie sheets. Bake in a 375° oven for 6 minutes. Immediately top each cookie with a mint. Bake for 1 to 2 minutes more or till cookies are light brown around edges. Swirl melted mints on cookies. Cool completely on a wire rack. Makes about 36 cookies.

Little Snow People

Cheerful snow people you can build indoors! (Pictured on page 15.)

1 **portion Festive Cookie Dough (see recipe, opposite)**
Miniature semisweet chocolate pieces
Red cinnamon candies
¾ **cup sifted powdered sugar**
Milk *or* light cream
Several drops green food coloring
Milk chocolate kisses *or* bite-size chocolate-covered peanut butter cups, halved
Sifted powdered sugar

If frozen, thaw Festive Cookie Dough in the refrigerator overnight. *Or,* place dough in a microwave-safe mixing bowl. Cover with waxed paper. Micro-cook on 10% power (low) about 5 minutes or till thawed, turning dough over once.

For each snow person, shape the dough into 3 balls: one 1-inch ball, one ¾-inch ball, and one ½-inch ball. Place on ungreased cookie sheet in order of decreasing sizes with edges touching. Press together slightly. Press 2 chocolate pieces in the smallest ball for eyes. Press 1 red cinnamon candy in the middle ball and 2 candies in the largest ball for buttons. Repeat with remaining dough to make additional snow people. Bake in a 325° oven about 18 minutes or till bottoms of cookies are light brown. Let stand for 1 minute on cookie sheets. Remove and cool completely on wire racks.

For icing, stir together the ¾ cup powdered sugar and enough milk or light cream (2 to 3 teaspoons) to make of piping consistency. Stir in the green food coloring. To make hats, use icing to attach halved kisses or peanut butter cups to small balls. Pipe bow ties, belts, scarves, or stocking caps on the snow people. Lightly sprinkle with the powdered sugar. Makes about 16 cookies.

13

Zigzag Cookie Shapes

1 **portion Festive Cookie Dough (see recipe, page 12)**
1 **cup sifted powdered sugar**
¼ **teaspoon vanilla**
  Milk
  Several drops red food coloring
  Several drops green food coloring

If frozen, thaw dough in the refrigerator overnight. *Or,* place in a microwave-safe bowl. Cover with waxed paper. Micro-cook on 10% power (low) about 5 minutes or till thawed, turning dough over once.

On a lightly floured surface, roll dough to ⅛-inch thickness. Cut with 2½-inch cookie cutters. Place on ungreased cookie sheets. Bake in a 375° oven for 6 to 8 minutes or till light brown around edges. Cool. For glaze, combine sugar, vanilla, and enough milk (3 to 4 teaspoons) to make of piping consistency. Divide glaze in half. Mix red food coloring in one half. Mix green food coloring in other half. Pipe both colors over cookies. Makes about 36 cookies.

Pecan Rounds

1 **portion Festive Cookie Dough (see recipe, page 12)**
1 **cup chopped pecans, toasted**
  Sugar

If frozen, thaw dough in the refrigerator overnight. *Or,* place in a microwave-safe bowl. Cover with waxed paper. Micro-cook on 10% power (low) about 5 minutes or till thawed, turning dough over once.

If necessary, let dough stand at room temperature for 20 minutes. Stir in pecans. Shape into 1-inch balls. Roll in sugar. Place on ungreased cookie sheets. Slightly flatten each with a glass dipped in sugar. Bake in a 375° oven for 7 to 9 minutes or till firm. Cool. Makes 36 cookies.

Clockwise from top left: Crackled Crescents, Zigzag Cookie Shapes, and Little Snow People (see recipe, page 13).

Crackled Crescents

1 portion Festive Cookie Dough (see recipe, page 12)
1 6-ounce package (1 cup) miniature semisweet chocolate pieces
1 tablespoon shortening Chopped coconut *or* finely chopped pistachio nuts

If frozen, thaw dough in the refrigerator overnight. *Or,* place in a microwave-safe bowl. Cover with waxed paper. Micro-cook on 10% power (low) about 5 minutes or till thawed, turning dough over once.

If necessary, let dough stand for 20 minutes. Stir in ½ *cup* of the chocolate pieces. Shape into 1-inch balls. Roll into 2-inch logs. Place on ungreased cookie sheets. Shape into crescents. Bake in a 375° oven for 8 to 10 minutes or till firm. Cool. Melt together remaining chocolate and shortening. Dip cookie ends into chocolate mixture. Roll in coconut or nuts. Chill till chocolate is set. Makes 36 cookies.

Oatmeal Cookie Mix

3½ cups all-purpose flour
2 cups packed brown
   sugar
1 cup sugar
2 teaspoons baking
   powder
¾ teaspoon salt
½ teaspoon baking soda
1½ cups shortening*
4 cups regular rolled oats

In a very large mixing bowl stir together flour, brown sugar, sugar, baking powder, salt, and baking soda. Cut in shortening till mixture resembles fine crumbs. Stir in oats. Store tightly covered at room temperature for up to 6 weeks. To measure, lightly spoon mix into a measuring cup and level with a spatula. Makes about 12 cups.

*Use shortening that *does not* need refrigeration.

Toffee-Oatmeal Cookies

Candy and cookie rolled into one! (Pictured on the cover and on page 19.)

2 slightly beaten eggs
¼ cup milk
1 teaspoon vanilla
4 cups Oatmeal Cookie
   Mix (see recipe,
   above)
3 1⅛-ounce bars
   chocolate-covered
   English toffee,
   crushed, *or* ¾ cup
   candy-coated milk
   chocolate pieces

In a mixing bowl stir together eggs, milk, and vanilla. Stir in cookie mix till combined. Stir in candy and, if desired, ½ cup broken *walnuts*. Drop by rounded tablespoons or ¼-cup portions onto lightly greased cookie sheets. Bake in a 375° oven till bottoms are light brown. (Allow 8 to 10 minutes for small cookies and 11 to 13 minutes for large cookies.) Let stand on cookie sheets for 1 minute. Remove and cool on wire racks. Makes about 27 small or 12 large cookies.

Easy Chocolate-Oatmeal Bars

Cut these into small bars because they're too rich to eat in large portions. (Pictured on page 19.)

1 **slightly beaten egg**
2 **tablespoons milk**
1 **teaspoon vanilla**
4 **cups Oatmeal Cookie Mix (see recipe, opposite)**
⅔ **cup semisweet chocolate pieces**
½ **cup Eagle Brand sweetened condensed milk**
1 **tablespoon margarine**
¼ **cup chopped walnuts**
1 **teaspoon vanilla**

In a mixing bowl stir together egg, 2 tablespoons milk, and 1 teaspoon vanilla. Stir in cookie mix till crumbly. Pat *two-thirds* of the mixture into a 9x9x2-inch baking pan.

In a small saucepan stir together chocolate pieces, ½ cup condensed milk, and margarine. Cook and stir over low heat till chocolate melts. Stir in walnuts and 1 teaspoon vanilla. Spread over oatmeal mixture in the pan. Dot with remaining oatmeal mixture. Bake in a 350° oven for 20 to 25 minutes or till set and light brown. Cool completely on a wire rack. Makes 25 bars.

Ginger-Oatmeal Cookies

1 **slightly beaten egg**
¼ **cup milk**
3 **tablespoons molasses**
1 **teaspoon ground ginger**
1 **teaspoon vanilla**
⅛ **teaspoon ground cloves**
4 **cups Oatmeal Cookie Mix (see recipe, opposite)**

In a mixing bowl stir together egg, milk, molasses, ginger, vanilla, and cloves. Stir in cookie mix till combined. Drop by rounded tablespoons or ¼-cup portions onto lightly greased cookie sheets. Bake in a 375° oven till bottoms are brown. (Allow 8 to 10 minutes for small cookies and 11 to 13 minutes for large cookies.) Let stand on cookie sheets for 1 minute. Remove and cool on wire racks. Makes about 27 small cookies or 12 large cookies.

Homemade Sugar Cookie Mix

Store the mix for up to six months in the freezer.

4 **cups all-purpose flour**
2 **cups sugar**
2 **teaspoons baking
    powder**
¾ **teaspoon salt**
1⅓ **cups shortening***

In a very large mixing bowl stir together flour, sugar, baking powder, and salt. Cut in shortening till mixture resembles fine crumbs. Store tightly covered at room temperature for up to 6 weeks. To measure, lightly spoon mix into a measuring cup and level with a spatula. Makes about 8½ cups.

*Use shortening that *does not* need refrigeration.

Orange-Coconut Drops

Use just four ingredients plus the cookie mix for these soft, fat cookies.

¼ **cup orange marmalade**
1 **egg**
3 **tablespoons orange
    juice**
2½ **cups Homemade Sugar
    Cookie Mix (see
    recipe, above)**
1 **cup coconut**

In a mixing bowl stir together marmalade, egg, and orange juice. Stir in cookie mix till combined. Stir in coconut. Drop from a rounded teaspoon onto lightly greased cookie sheets. Bake in a 350° oven for 8 to 10 minutes or till brown around edges. Let stand on cookie sheets for 1 minute. Remove and cool on wire racks. Makes about 32 cookies.

Clockwise from top: Toffee-Oatmeal Cookies (see recipe, page 16), Fresh-Fruit Cookie Tarts (see recipe, page 22), Easy Chocolate-Oatmeal Bars (see recipe, page 17), and Orange-Coconut Drops.

Peanut Butter and Jelly Cookies

⅓ cup peanut butter
1 egg
½ teaspoon vanilla
2½ cups Homemade Sugar
    Cookie Mix (see
    recipe, opposite)
    Sugar
    Grape jelly

In a mixer bowl combine peanut butter, egg, and vanilla; beat till fluffy. Add cookie mix; beat till well combined. Shape dough into 1-inch balls. Roll in sugar. Place 2 inches apart on ungreased cookie sheets. Press down centers with your thumb.

Bake in a 375° oven about 10 minutes or till golden brown around the edges. Let stand on cookie sheets for 1 minute. Remove and cool on wire racks.

Just before serving, fill center of each cookie with ½ teaspoon grape jelly. Makes about 36 cookies.

Cereal-Peanut-Butter Bars

Peanut butter and chocolate: an all-American flavor combination.

½ cup light corn syrup
¼ cup packed brown
    sugar
    Dash salt
1 cup peanut butter
1 teaspoon vanilla
2 cups crisp rice cereal
1 cup slightly crushed
    cornflakes
1 6-ounce package
    (1 cup) semisweet
    chocolate pieces

Butter a 9x9x2-inch baking pan. Set aside. In a medium saucepan combine light corn syrup, brown sugar, and salt. Bring to boiling, stirring constantly. Stir in peanut butter. Remove from the heat. Stir in vanilla. Stir in rice cereal, cornflakes, and chocolate pieces. Press into the prepared pan. Cover and chill till firm. Store in the refrigerator. Makes 24 bars.

Bran New Chews

½ cup packed brown
    sugar
⅓ cup light corn syrup
¾ cup chunk-style peanut
    butter
2 cups bran cereal
    squares, slightly
    crushed
⅓ cup raisins

In a medium saucepan stir together brown sugar and corn syrup. Bring to boiling, stirring constantly. Remove from the heat. Stir in peanut butter till combined. Stir in cereal and raisins till well coated. Drop by rounded teaspoons onto cookie sheets lined with waxed paper. (*Or,* press mixture evenly into a foil-lined 8x8x2-inch pan.) Cool till firm. Store in a covered container. Makes about 24 cookies or 24 bars.

Rudolph's Antlers

Shape cookie mixture into antler pairs, topping each set with a cherry half for Rudolph's red nose.

½ **of a 6-ounce package (½ cup) butterscotch pieces**
½ **teaspoon shortening**
1 **6-ounce package (1 cup) semisweet chocolate pieces**
1 **3-ounce can (2 cups) chow mein noodles**
12 **maraschino cherries, halved (optional)**

In a medium saucepan heat butterscotch pieces and shortening over low heat till almost melted, stirring occasionally. Add chocolate pieces and continue heating and stirring till chocolate is melted. Remove from the heat. Stir in chow mein noodles. Drop by rounded teaspoons onto a cookie sheet lined with waxed paper, making V-shape cookies about 2 inches long. Place a cherry half in the center of each. Chill in the refrigerator till cookies are firm. Store, covered, in the refrigerator. Makes about 24 cookies.

Chocolate Drop Cookies

2 **cups sugar**
¼ **cup unsweetened cocoa powder**
½ **cup milk**
½ **cup margarine *or* butter**
1 **tablespoon light corn syrup**
¼ **cup peanut butter**
2 **cups quick-cooking rolled oats**

In a heavy 3-quart saucepan stir together sugar and cocoa powder. Stir in milk. Add margarine or butter and corn syrup. Bring to boiling, stirring occasionally. Boil vigorously for 3 minutes. Remove from the heat. Stir in peanut butter. Stir in rolled oats.

Return mixture to heat. Bring to boiling. Remove from heat; beat till mixture mounds slightly when dropped from a spoon. Immediately drop by rounded teaspoons onto cookie sheets lined with waxed paper. (If mixture spreads too much, beat a little longer.) Cool till firm. Makes about 36 cookies.

Apricot-Oatmeal Bars

1 roll refrigerated
   oatmeal-raisin *or*
   sugar cookie dough
1 12-ounce can apricot
   cake and pastry
   filling
½ cup broken walnuts
   or pecans
1 tablespoon lemon juice

Let cookie dough stand at room temperature while preparing filling. For filling, stir together apricot filling, walnuts or pecans, and lemon juice.

Pat *two-thirds* of the cookie dough into an ungreased 9x9x2-inch baking pan. Spread apricot mixture over the dough. Dot with the remaining cookie dough. Bake in a 375° oven for 20 to 25 minutes or till light brown. Cool completely. Makes 24 bars.

Fresh-Fruit Cookie Tarts

Fruit and cream cheese top individual cookie rounds. (Pictured on page 19.)

1 roll refrigerated
   oatmeal-raisin,
   peanut butter, *or*
   sugar cookie dough
   Desired fruit such as
   strawberries,
   bananas, seedless
   grapes, oranges,
   kiwi fruits, *or* apples
1 8-ounce container
   soft-style cream
   cheese with fruit
   Raisins *or* toasted
   coconut (optional)

Cut cookie dough roll into 8 slices. Place 4 inches apart on ungreased cookie sheets. Use your hand to flatten each slice into a 2½-inch circle. Bake in a 375° oven for 9 to 11 minutes or till cookies are light golden brown. Cool completely on a wire rack.

Before serving, cut up desired fruit. Spread about *1 rounded tablespoon* cream cheese on *each* cookie. Top with cut-up fruit. If desired, sprinkle with raisins or coconut. Makes 8 cookies.

Craters of Coconut

Don't press the dough into the pans. It spreads on its own. (Pictured on page 5.)

1 roll refrigerated sugar
  cookie dough
3 tablespoons brown
  sugar
1 tablespoon margarine
  or butter, softened
1 tablespoon milk
⅓ cup coconut
½ cup finely chopped nuts

Cut dough into 9 slices. Cut each slice into fourths. Place pieces of dough in lightly greased 1¾-inch-diameter muffin pans. Bake in a 350° oven for 8 to 10 minutes or till edges are light brown. Meanwhile, stir together brown sugar and margarine or butter. Add milk; mix well. Stir in coconut and nuts.

Remove muffin pans from oven. Put about *1 rounded teaspoon* of the coconut mixture in the center of *each* partially baked cookie. Bake in the 350° oven about 3 minutes more or till edges are golden brown. Cool in pans for 10 minutes. Carefully remove cookies from pans. Cool on wire racks. Makes 36 cookies.

Cherry-Chocolate Bars

1 roll refrigerated double
  chocolate cookie
  dough
½ cup chopped walnuts
1 8-ounce container
  soft-style cream
  cheese (plain)
1 21-ounce can cherry
  pie filling

Spread cookie dough in an ungreased 11x7x1½-inch baking pan. Sprinkle with walnuts. Bake in a 350° oven for 18 to 20 minutes or till a wooden toothpick inserted near the center comes out clean. Cool completely on a wire rack. Spread cream cheese over the top. Top with cherry pie filling. Store in the refrigerator. Makes 12 bars.

INDEX